CW01667107

NURSE, GIVE ME A PILL FOR DEATH

by Aldona Grupas

EURASIAN CREATIVE GUILD
LONDON

HERTFORDSHIRE PRESS

Printed in United Kingdom
Cambridge International Press
Imprint of Hertfordshire Press Ltd © 2018
e-mail: publisher@hertfordshirepress.com
www.hertfordshirepress.com

On behalf of Eurasian Creative Guild, London

EURASIAN CREATIVE GUILD LONDON

NURSE, GIVE ME A PILL FOR DEATH

by Aldona Grupas ©

English

Edited by David Stanford
Illustrations by Artsiom Albach
Typeset by Alexandra Rey

British Library Catalogue in Publication Data
A catalogue record for this book is available from the British Library
Library of Congress in Publication Data
A catalogue record for this book has been requested

ISBN: 978-1-910886-92-2

CONTENTS

PREFACE

Time rushes by faster than we realise. Three years ago, I wrote and published a book titled *The Lithuanian Community of the West Midlands of England after the Second World War (1947–2012)*. It revealed how difficult it was for my Lithuanian compatriots to start out in England, finding their place and finally settling here. For them, England was a very strange community – but they managed in the end.

I would like to highlight the existence of that book, particularly for Lithuanians living in England. If you fall into this category, maybe reading the book will cause you to reminisce? Maybe you will remember relatives from years ago who have been lost in other countries over the years? Maybe you would like to tell me something – your story perhaps? Let's communicate; I'm ready and waiting to hear from you.

I am very grateful to those British Lithuanians who have entrusted their family stories to me, who told about the adventures of their parents, about them going to a foreign country, which became their second homeland.

For those who would ask me why I wrote such a book – bearing in mind that writing is not my vocation – I would like to clarify my motivation. I am simply in love with those people who, while living in a foreign country, are able to remain free, protecting and preserving Lithuania's heritage, preserving the culture and traditions inherited from their ancestors. For me, they set the greatest example.

As a nurse, my job is very different from that of a creative writer, but writing has never been alien to me. I was never a stranger to the pain of others, and I was always curious, asking: "How did everything start?"

When I came to England and met the active Lithuanian community, I asked myself: "Where was the beginning? How did my compatriots feel in a foreign land? How did they stabilize and find security here? How did they protect their Lithuanian culture?"

Having talked to a few of them, I realized that, although everything was not easy, some very beautiful things also happened. I felt that all this valuable information should not be wasted, and I found it necessary to write everything down and bring this information to others.

Now I have written a second book: *Nurse, Give Me a Death Pill.* It is about my own journey to England in search of a nursing career, a search that was at times difficult and frustrating. It is also about my experience of adjusting to life in England, learning to communicate in a new language and adapting to new professional practices. There were many bumps in the road – including distrust and discrimination – but I got there in the end, and the experience has been enriching.

This new book also explores an important aspect of my professional work: caring for people with terminal illness and the elderly, who often face many struggles before departing from this world. I am one of those people who help the very sick, trying to ease their daily existence, holding the hands of those who must learn to accept the sunset of their lives. I have tried to show what it takes to survive in an environment saturated with hopelessness and death.

When I first moved to England, I worked as a care assistant, later registering as a nurse, which is my current job. Without nurses and care assistants, many people would have much more difficult lives, particularly in their final years.

This new book reflects the fact that many nurses and care assistants recognize the value of their jobs, feeling them to be more than just work; rather, it is a vocation, something that brings meaning to their lives. Over a period of more than ten years, my nursing career really became my life, and the people who I worked with became my second family.

To illustrate this point, I have also included some observations from other nurses – including some colleagues of mine – showing how deeply they feel about their profession and the contribution they can make to helping others in need.

Among those contributing to this book and supporting my efforts is my friend and fellow nurse Audrone Lamb. Another nurse, Galina Hartshorn, has also made an invaluable contribution. Galina is a Proctor and Gallagher Institute coach and she lectures in personal development at Nottingham Hospital. I offer my sincere thanks to them and to my other female friends and collaborators who inspired me to tell my own story and those of other nurses who have travelled to foreign countries to pursue their careers.

Writing this book also led me to meet Bob Proctor, a world-famous personal-development teacher and the author of the bestseller "You Were Born Rich". Among the inspirational passages in his book is this one: "Thoughts become things. If you see it in your mind, you will hold it in your hand."

Let's face it, if we continue to think about the difficulties that lie ahead, fearing that we will not be able to overcome them, we will attract an even greater problem: loss of confidence. So, what can we do to make life less troublesome?

Proctor tells us that the path containing all our encountered difficulties is a simple path and we shouldn't get confused and blame ourselves if things don't go according to plan. Who knows, maybe the deviation from the original plan will lead to a better outcome?

According to Proctor, to make life uncomplicated, and to remove the difficulties, you need to expel all bad thoughts from your mind. Instead, he says, you need to enjoy life, to look forward to it and to believe in it.

I have noticed that Proctor's philosophy is very close to my own philosophy, and when I use it, I am much happier. I feel happy when I believe in myself and when I believe in what I do. Of course, I have had – and still have – many good counsellors and advisors in whom I also believe and trust. To them, I offer my continued thanks.

I present this new book to you – my readers – hoping

that you will enjoy it. I also wish you good luck in life and hopefulness in everything you do.

Chapter I

DREAMS COME TRUE

"Dreams come true when desire transforms into concrete actions. Ask a lot from life and life will give you a lot."
– Napoleon Hil

I was born in Riga, Latvia, but I spent my summers at my grandmother's village in Lithuania. As a child, I dreamed about living in Lithuania too. I dreamed; I asked my parents; I begged my guardian angel – I prayed to God for my wishes to be fulfilled. And finally, that day came.

However, after many years in Lithuania, my life changed again. I had foreign friends and began to travel abroad, initially to Poland and then to Germany. When I travelled to West Germany, I was astounded by the differences between the two countries. Commuting annually to Germany to visit friends, I started to dream about life abroad. Friends gave me the idea that maybe I could go to live in Germany.

I was a trained nurse, having qualified back in 1979, and my husband was a doctor. I had worked as a medical sister, but the pay was poor, so I had gone into business, opening my own beauty salon. My husband and I knew that there was great demand for medical professionals in other countries, and the idea of living abroad appealed to us both. My husband liked Germany, but he refused to go there, largely because he couldn't speak the German language. He said he would go only to English-speaking countries. So again, I began dreaming of going to another country – although I was not sure where that might be.

In 2005, I was a part-time law student at the Riga Law Institute of Klaipeda. Lectures were held four nights a week, with most of the students holding jobs on the side. After the lectures, I would often meet with colleagues in a popular café called Chilli Pizza. We discussed our work, our lives, and our futures.

I will never forget one meeting in particular. I was talking with Ula, a fourth-year student, about the uncertain future of the Institute and its qualifications, and how this left me and the other students in an ambiguous situation. At the time, there were rumours that Lithuania was considering not recognizing our law diplomas, which would mean all our study would have been for nothing. You study, you learn, and you earn a diploma – and then it's not worth the paper it's printed on. What a shame! A lawyer without a diploma won't get anywhere.

However, I said that I was an optimist, and no matter what happened, I would be okay. After all, I was already a trained nurse.

I still, to this day, remember the surprised response of Ula.

"You are a nurse?" she said. "What are you doing here? You already have a good profession! Drive to England; they need nurses there. You will earn a good living!"

I was shaken by those words and the manner in which they were expressed. I had never imagined that I could just drive to England and find work. When I got home, I told my husband what my good friend had said. He was not at all surprised. He said that a friend of ours – another doctor – was using intermediaries in Lithuania to help him search for a job in the United Kingdom. He was attending English-language classes for doctors in Vilnius.

What a coincidence! I had been dreaming of working abroad, and now I had been told how to go about it. The answer had been handed to me on a silver platter.

My husband became infected with my fire and determination. Through his friend, we started making preparations for him to find work as a doctor in England, contacting various organizations that provided the required courses.

That weekend, we agreed to see with our own eyes how the English courses were run. The course we attended was advanced, aimed at providing doctors with the English skills necessary to communicate with patients and colleagues. The students were also advanced, having already taken primer courses. I had studied some English at the Institute in Lithuania, a branch of the University of Latvia, and so I was not a beginner. However, dropping right into that advanced course was not easy. I had to learn a lot of new medical terms in English and how to use those terms when conversing with patients.

That said, the lessons were interesting and we were warmly accepted. We soon became more closely acquainted with our new colleagues, some of whom are still friends to this day. In the evenings, we had barbecue outings and karaoke parties where we communicated only in English. It was fun and very useful to speak in English in an informal setting.

We established links with an agency in the UK that specialised in finding work there for doctors. When my husband contacted the agency, they immediately began to search for a job for him, while preparing the necessary documents. As a nurse, I was not able to benefit from their assistance, so I turned my attention elsewhere, researching various agencies that dealt specifically with nurses.

I was very cautions, because I had read many sad stories in the press about people who had been defrauded by dishonest agencies. I later met people in England who had suffered in this way. They told me that some agencies advertised jobs, took money from their customers, transported them to England, and then disappeared, leaving the customers stranded. I realized that I could only rely upon serious organizations.

Searching through the newspaper advertisements, I found a firm in Vilnius that said it could help me find employment in England with Bupa, a well-known private healthcare company. I did my research on Bupa, and after reviewing the work offered – and learning that the agency would not charge me for their services – I decided to sign up.

I was invited to Vilnius for an interview, which would be conducted over the phone with a potential employer in England. I had never spoken English on the telephone before, and I was so nervous that all my knowledge of the language evaporated. Of course, I was not successful.

As I was so determined to leave Lithuania for England, I took a risk, signing up with an agency that charged for its services. Once I made the payment, I began to receive calls from potential employers in England who were interested in hearing about my nursing experience.

I concentrated, and this time, I was able to speak English much better, answering their various questions. The calls were long and we spoke a lot. Sometimes I got my words mixed up, but my confidence grew stronger, and I spoke better as the conversations became longer. I look back today at those conversations and I smile: "Well, I was stubborn."

Not long after, I received another call from the agency. They said that they had found a job for me and I should prepare to move to England soon. I was worried about what lay in store for me, but I calmed down a little when I learned that the job was near London. If it turned out to be a scam and I was left on the street, I would be able to contact some of my Lithuanian acquaintances living in London and stay with them for a while.

I hastily packed my suitcases. My husband did not try to dissuade me. We decided that if we waited until he was offered a job in England, it might be too late for me.

I consoled myself with the following reasoning: "I'm going first; I'll have a look around, and then he will come later."

Chapter II

FOGGY ALBION

For those of you who do not know – or may have forgotten – I would like to describe a place called "Albion". There is no country of that name in the modern world; it cannot be found on modern maps. Rather, Albion is an ancient name for Britain, that island comprised of the modern nations of England, Scotland and Wales.

Albion means "White Land", probably a reference to the spectacular White Cliffs of Dover, which visitors (or invaders) would have seen on arrival by boat. Some people, however, believe it refers to the foggy weather for which Britain is famous.

The name is thought to be Celtic in origin, derived from "albus", the Latin word for "white". It was first mentioned in ancient Greek sources during the fifth or sixth century BC. The Romans, who invaded England in AD 43, used the name Albion, although their own name for the place – "Britain" – later prevailed.

Albion to this day is used as a poetic name for England. It was widely prevalent in nineteenth century fiction and I must admit to liking it. It has an appealing, mysterious sound, suggestive of old castles, mist-shrouded valleys and allegedly supernatural phenomena. It was to this "Foggy Albion" that I was determined to go.

When I had first signed up with the agency in Lithuania, I fully expected that my work would be in London or one of its suburbs. However, as my day of departure came closer, I learned that the job was somewhere quite different – in the northern city of Leeds. Before boarding the plane to London, I spoke with a woman from the agency who gave me the address in Leeds. She said that the people there would organize my documents and direct me to my workplace.

I travelled to "my Albion" for the first time on 23 August, 2005, arriving alone at London's Stansted Airport. As I mingled with the people in the crowded airport and listened to them speaking, I felt like I'd been hit over the head.

"This is England?" I thought. "What language are they speaking? This is not the language that I learned!"

Such was my first impression of the various dialects around me; I seemed to be swamped in a sea of foreign-speaking people. Luckily, at the airport information office, I was able to communicate in English and understand what I was told.

Everything was new to me and there was a lot of excitement, but I realized that I had to concentrate and think about what to do, where to go and what I needed. The journey to my first place of work was going to be long and intricate, and I had to focus.

I bought a bus ticket and started on my journey to Leeds, which was not at all close. I travelled all night, and on arrival I took a taxi to the agency's office. At the agency, people were arriving from everywhere and their objective was the same as mine: to get a job. I didn't meet anyone from Lithuania.

At the office, I learned that I would work as a nurse's assistant – also called a "care assistant". I would be paid the minimum wage, which was £4.85 in England at that time. I was disappointed that I was not being offered work as a qualified nurse. In Lithuania I had worked as medical sister, and I was convinced that I would immediately get similar work in England. I did not understand yet that the English health system was very different from the Lithuanian, that I must overcome various obstacles to reach my goal.

I was told that I would be working in Southport, a city on the west coast of England, 17 miles north of Liverpool. I was very surprised that I was being sent to Southport because the agency had not mentioned the place at all.

I called the woman from the Lithuanian agency to find out what was happening. Why was I being offered poorly-paid care-assistant work? She explained that I would have to go back to London, where another agent would meet me and explain everything. Before heading back down to London, however, I had to complete the employment documents at the office in Leeds. This took all day, so I was obliged to stay overnight at a hotel.

The next morning, I journeyed back down to London. While I was on the bus, I received a call from a man who spoke in English. I wasn't quite sure who he was, but he was unhappy that I was not taking the job in Southport. He offered to meet me at Euston railway station in London, where we would discuss my options. I did not understand anything that was going on – but I had to trust him.

We met at Euston as arranged, and it became clear that he was the manager of the agency in Lithuania. He said that I should take the job I was offered in Southport, and using my money, he bought me a train ticket for the next day. He said I could spend the night in an empty cottage on the outskirts of London, an area mostly inhabited by newcomers from Asia.

Just to make my situation more complicated, as I was preparing to return to Southport, I received a phone call from someone offering me a job in London. The man on the phone said the job was mine if I wanted it; all I had to do was get on a bus to the workplace. He was even willing to pay for my ticket across London. It was very tempting, but I declined the offer. After all, who was to know whether it would be better or worse than Southport?

My thoughts were racing by now. I knew the agent's communications to be poor, so I wasn't so surprised to find some confusion over where I would be working. But I faced another problem: Where was London? Apparently, I was in London already, but I felt like I hadn't really seen it. My impressions of the city were based solely on Euston Station and the area in which I stayed overnight.

Of course, I didn't have time to think too deeply about London and how it looked. I was thinking only about my own safety, and about tomorrow's trip to Southport, where my new job was waiting for me. Despite the confusion and various difficulties, I was accompanied everywhere by a silent feeling of joy; after all, I had not yet been cheated or left alone on the street.

Yes, there had been some confusion, but everything was working out just right. Looking back, I don't regret a single moment of those first few days. After all, I'm an optimist, and I believe in Fate. Wherever Fate leads you is where you're meant to be.

Chapter III

LIKE A KITTEN IN WATER

In Southport, I was given accommodation shared by employees at the same place of work. The workers were of various nationalities, and I was very happy to discover that among them was a Lithuanian woman. I shared a room with an Icelandic woman who enjoyed chatting, and I was happy for the opportunity to practice my English.

The day after I moved into my lodgings, I was given directions to my new place of work. I went there to get acquainted with my workplace – a small, private nursing home for elderly people. The manager was cold, but she introduced me to a Lithuanian woman who worked there, instructing her to show me my duties.

These involved the daily care of the residents, including feeding, washing and dressing them, taking them to the bathroom, and monitoring their skin and health conditions. Any status changes had to be reported to the nurse. Care assistants were not required to manhandle the patients. For this purpose, there were special lifting devices called hoists or standing aids. I appreciated that what was being asked of me, was a serious and responsible job.

There were three Lithuanians working in the nursing home: two women and a young man. We became friends and have stayed in contact since then. One of the Lithuanians, a woman named Jolanta, was a qualified nurse. She explained that the facility employed people as care assistants rather than nurses, regardless of their qualifications.

In order to work as a nurse, she said, I would have to apply to the Nursing and Midwifery Council (NMC) for a professional qualification number (PIN). Only then could I start applying for real nursing jobs in England. In Lithuania, I already had my nursing license, but to get my PIN in the UK, I would need to get various documents sent over from Vilnius.

The manager at the nursing home said that I would be summoned to work as soon as they had checked my criminal history. I had already provided the results of a criminal-record check from Lithuania. However, the rules required that a further check be conducted using the UK's own criminal-records database.

The situation was somewhat different for people who already had the appropriate professional registration in the UK – such as qualified nurses with a PIN. In such cases, no questions were asked about a possible criminal record.

It took over a week for my UK criminal-record check to be completed. As I waited, not knowing when I would begin work, I wondered how I would survive with no income. I felt like a kitten paddling about in a river, struggling to keep its head above water. There was no telling whether I would make a success of this move to a strange country.

The good news was that in England at that time – at least in the Southport area – one could do all one's grocery shopping on just £15 a week. In the Asda supermarket, where I usually shopped, it was possible to buy good food at a very low price. I wondered why Lithuania was not like this.

With a lot of free time on my hands, I walked around the town in order to get acquainted with the English way of living. Many things surprised me. For one thing, I saw many people walking around the streets in their work uniforms. There were people dressed as sales assistants and bar staff, for example, as well as nurses. In England, it seemed that no one changed from their uniforms into their normal clothes when they left work.

I was particularly puzzled by the doctors and nurses, wearing the same white uniforms on the streets as they had worn in clinical settings. To me, this did not look right. It was also contrary to the requirements of sanitation, which is an important factor when working with sick and injured people. After a while, I also became a part of that crowd, but I never let myself be seen outside of my working environment wearing my working clothes.

There was also inconsistency in dress codes, with many doctors working without their medical coats, wearing casual clothes instead. At the nursing home where I worked, it was often impossible to distinguish between a doctor and an everyday visitor.

England is a tolerant country, affording basic rights to its diverse and multi-ethnic workforce. However, some of the sights were a surprise to me, newly arrived from Lithuania. For example, I had never before seen doctors wearing headscarves and floor-sweeping skirts. Nor had I seen Indian doctors wearing turbans in their offices. It was good to know that they changed their clothes before entering the operating rooms. In England, as everywhere else in the world, the same rule applies: the theatre must be sterile.

In the following years, I would work in various retirement homes, nursing homes and hospitals, and I learned that infectious diseases – including MRSA and scabies – are fairly common. Indeed, it is still the case that patients often pick up infections at hospitals and other medical facilities in England.

Chapter IV

MY FIRST WORKPLACE

At last, I was summoned to start work. It was only my first day on the job, but already I was confronted with a new shock. Many of the nursing-home residents spoke in a regional dialect of English, and for this reason I was assigned to work with another Lithuanian.

I had to admit that I could not understand what the residents were saying. It was explained to me later that they were speaking with a Liverpool accent, which even the British have difficulty with. Added to which, of course, the English that I had learned in Lithuania was far from perfect.

However, I set to my work with enthusiasm and in the following weeks I began to get the hang of things. Due to the constant need for communication with the residents, and also with my colleagues, my knowledge of the English language improved rapidly. In the process, I learned a great deal about English cuisine and eating habits, as well as the daily routines, way of life and the traditions of the people.

I gave myself an added boost by signing up for college and attending English-language courses.

I also had to attend college courses in nursing practice. These covered health-and-safety issues, such as patient safety and the correct methods for lifting patients. Despite the emphasis on the safety of care assistants, there were still occasional incidents at work, including back injuries. We were instructed in the use of special lifting equipment to try to reduce such incidents. We were also shown various nursing measures that required specialist knowledge. Overall, I was impressed with the range of measures to facilitate the work of nursing staff and ensure patient safety in England.

One thing I was not impressed with, however, was the rule that care assistants working in nursing homes must operate in pairs, even when not required to physically move a patient. The rule is based on the principle that there should always be a third person in any care situation who can provide evidence in case of claims of wrong-doing. This rule is designed to protect patients from mistreatment, but also to protect staff from unfair allegations.

In my job, this rule became a problem whenever we had a shortage of staff. It would have been helpful if the care assistants were allowed to perform certain tasks alone, but this was not permitted, and it often slowed us down. Such rules did not apply in Lithuania, and I found myself getting quite upset at the situation I now found myself in. In Lithuania, I had worked in a clinic and later in a sanatorium. There I took the attitude that all jobs, no matter how menial, had to be done – with or without additional help.

It is commonly said that the work of a care assistant can be exhausting, low-paid and not fully appreciated. This first job in England fitted this description well. There was a lot to be done each day, including physical tasks such as washing, dressing and feeding the residents. I will describe these tasks in more detail later in the book. For now, let me just say how glad I was to have started work in England at last. My English dream was finally becoming a reality, for which I was truly grateful.

Chapter V

A SECOND ATTEMPT

I worked for just three months in England before returning to Lithuania in the autumn of 2005. My husband was still waiting for a job offer in England, and I wanted to be with him.

I was only in Vilnius for a few days before I received a phone call from an agency. It was the same agency that had supplied me with my first – and disastrous – telephone interview. They wondered whether my English had improved, and if I was still looking for work.

After all my practice in Southport, I easily impressed them with my English over the phone. They invited me to a meeting in Vilnius with a prospective employer: Bupa. The interview with the Bupa representative went so well that, as I sat there in the office, I already knew that I would get the job.

I was pleased with the outcome, but this time I didn't want to go to England by myself. I told the representative that my husband was looking for work as a doctor in England, and I wanted to wait for him to sign a contract before I relocated again. I said I was hoping to get a job in the same general location as my husband. The company agreed to my conditions. Now it was just a matter of waiting.

In 2006, my husband finally signed a contract for a job in Staffordshire, in the English West Midlands. To fit with his plans, Bupa offered me a one-year contract at one of their nursing homes in Walsall, not far from my husband's new job. It was all working out as planned, and very soon we were ready for departure.

Lithuanians moving to England to work for Bupa were normally met at the airport in London by a company representative. In this way, new arrivals were not required to wander about looking for transportation and accommodation; rather, they were taken direct to the right place and provided with somewhere to stay.

My husband and I were a little different, because we arrived in England by car, not aeroplane. However, Bupa was still very good in looking after us. We were settled into a hotel, all expenses paid, including food. Soon after that, a two-bedroom house was found for us. The deposit and half the rent were paid by the company. My husband and I were both getting free meals at work, so that helped reduce costs too.

I was very pleased by Bupa's sense of responsibility toward its employees. I still have work assignments at a Bupa nursing home sometimes, and so far as I know, they still treat their employees in this responsible manner.

I soon started work at the nursing home, where I was employed as a nursing assistant – basically the same role as I was performing in Southport. Once again, I found that communicating with the residents was a challenge at times, partly because my English still wasn't great. However, through my interactions with both staff and patients, I began to get more insight into British English – including some culturally specific expressions.

I met one resident, a very intelligent elderly man who had worked as a teacher, and we soon became friends. He taught me English pronunciation and awareness of various dialects. He also told me a variety of funny stories, enabling me to better understand English humour. In this way, he said, I would not be insulted by hearing ambiguous English expressions. To the uninitiated foreigner, such expressions can sometimes sound quite different from the intended meaning.

For example, English people like to address their friends, companions, acquaintances or even clients with sweet and nice-sounding words. However, at first, such expressions did not always seem appropriate to me. In English culture, it is common to address some as "love". In the Lithuanian language, calling someone "love" when you don't know them well would be considered an insult.

When I was first addressed in this way – by a Pakistani nurse – I was confused and angry.

"What kind of person am I to you?" I demanded.

I later realized that it was just a friendly English greeting – no more and no less.

I subsequently came to learn of many different words of greeting, some of them specific to particular regions of England, such as: "chick" (chicken), "duck" (duck), "cock" (buddy), "mate" (friend). All of the above are just friendly ways of addressing another person, and I was glad to have downloaded this crucial information.

The same topic was raised during a short nursing course that I was sent on when I started at the nursing home. Part of the course was about communicating with both patients and colleagues. We had to show respect and empathy, addressing patients with affectionate terms such as "love", "sweetheart", "dear" and "darling". In England, such terms are used everywhere – by shop cashiers, restaurant waiting staff, hospital nurses, and even the passers-by in the street, regardless of age.

I started taking English-language courses at a local college. I was studying alongside other English people, in a small group of just five students, all of whom were having problems with their own language. I was surprised to find that one of the students – a British person – was completely illiterate.

This man was a farmer and otherwise very capable and practical individual in full time employment. He studied individual letters of the alphabet to help him read. I found his problem with reading and writing to be quite unusual. It wasn't due to dyslexia, but rather from lack of education.

Another man was studying English in order to gain a higher position at work. He needed to pass the English exam and obtain a certificate at an appropriate level. The group also included two mentally retarded people.

Another peculiarity of the English language is the way that measures of time are used, which is quite different from the Lithuania approach. The English like to say, "Just a minute" or "It will only take a minute". Or else they say, "I will be there in a minute" or "I will do it in a minute." However, as I soon discovered, when an English person says they will be with you in a minute, they don't mean literally one minute. They mean they'll be there as soon as they can. Compared with Lithuanians, the British are usually not so prompt.

I also took some time to get my head around the different ways the word "problem" is also used – depending on whether there is a problem or there isn't. For example, sometimes it's used in response to expressions of gratitude. If someone says, "Thank you," the response is often, "No problem". This can mean that there really were no problems, or perhaps that there were some problems – but the person has no problem with the problems!

The work "alright" took a bit of getting used to as well. In one context, it means that everything is okay, but in another context it just means, "Good morning!"

I soon discovered that people of different nationalities behave quite differently in similar situations. The British, I found out, use many words to express gratitude and apology, which is not something Lithuanians would do. If you step on an ethnically British person's foot, they are more likely to say sorry than swear at you!

Of course, this does not necessarily mean that they want to be on friendly terms with you. They may even be uttering obscenities under their breath.

Learning how to apply a foreign language in conjunction with a nation's character, its customs and philosophy, can be problematical. But with a bit of effort and some help from those around me, I was slowly getting the hang of it.

Chapter VI

THE CARE ASSISTANT'S JOB

The job of a care assistant in a nursing home is not easy, involving both psychological and physical pressures. There is a lot to get done in the course of a working day, and one must always be attentive to the needs of the residents, regardless of the workload. Perhaps the best way of illustrating the challenges of the job is to show a typical care assistant's working day from start to end.

A full-time care assistant often works shifts of 12 hours or more, from 8am to 8pm or even 7am to 9pm. The key tasks for the day are assigned by a nurse or administrator of some kind, with one or more care assistants responsible for preparing breakfast, while others will dress the residents, and others give them a morning wash.

Breakfast is served to the residents according to their needs and wishes. Some residents will have their meals in their rooms, while others eat in the common areas. Some will be able to feed themselves and merely need the food delivered, while others will need help with the actual process of eating. In order to meet this array of needs, the kitchen staff and care assistants will divide the tasks, with some delivering food while others hand-feed the residents.

As with lunch and dinner, the residents are normally able to choose their preferred breakfast foods from a menu, with orders placed the previous day.

Washing and dressing is another crucial part of the morning routine. After the residents have been given a wash, they will be helped to dress, although some are quite able to do this for themselves. While care assistants often make suggestions on what to wear, the final decision rests with the resident, based on their own preferences. No matter how they want to dress, we will help them, providing as much or as little assistance as needed.

Once everyone has been dressed and fed, the staff will typically take a break of about 15 or 20 minutes. Then they will prepare the next important stage, which is a tea break for the residents at around 11am. This is a well-established British tradition and one that residents value highly. To quote the famous British Prime Minister William Gladstone: "Thank God for tea! What would the world be without tea! I am glad to be born after the discovery of tea."

As I learned early on, British people normally take milk in their tea; it's a rare person indeed who likes it black. The British usually cannot drink their tea without a biscuit of some sort, and so these are normally provided as a matter of course.

Tea breaks are also very important from a health point of view because elderly residents must get a certain quantity of liquids each day. Care assistants have to keep written records of the liquids that each resident consumes, including what was drunk, how much and when. This information is part of the patients' care plan, aimed at ensuring patient wellbeing.

Next on the care-assistant's list is lunch, followed by an afternoon tea break, and then at about 5pm comes dinner. Many British people refer to dinner as "tea time", while in Lithuania we called it "before dinner time". Once again, the residents are normally able to order their preferred dishes from a menu, and the same care is taken to ensure everyone gets properly fed. Some people only want a light dinner – such as crisps and sandwiches – although there are normally hot meals on the menu too.

Between 7pm and 8pm is "evening drinks" time. A range of hot beverages is usually served, including tea, hot chocolate, cocoa and Horlicks. If residents want a small snack later in the evening, this can also be arranged.

Once the final food and drinks have been served, it's time for some peace and quiet. Some residents will go to sleep, while others stay awake, enjoying a longer evening. Some prefer to watch television, while others read a book or chat with friends.

And so another day passes: get up, get dressed, eat, drink, spend the day, go to sleep.

Throughout the day, of course, residents also need to go to the toilet. It's part of the care assistant's job to help residents if they need help in the bathroom, including changing the diapers of those residents who use them.

Generally speaking, the amount of work that a care assistant puts in depends on the level of care that the residents require, with three categories identified in the UK. The first group includes residents who require minimal assistance or none at all. The second group consists of residents who are bedridden or unable to move their limbs. The third group includes people with mental disabilities: those suffering from dementia, Alzheimer's disease, or who have other serious psychological problems.

Of course, the schedule outlined above describes the work of care assistants during the day. For those working at night, things are slightly different. At night, every two hours, the assistant must visit the residents' rooms, verify that they are okay, and change their diapers if necessary. Among the other nocturnal duties are resident surveys and cleaning tasks.

In order to carry out the work of a care assistant properly, endless patience is required. If there is a lack of patience at first, it often develops over time. And this is just one way in which a person can be changed for the better in the course of doing the job. By helping an elderly person, many care assistants become more intelligent, tolerant and patient, adapting to the needs of others, and learning how to satisfy those needs.

Chapter VII

A CLASH WITH MANAGEMENT

When I was working in Lithuania, I was told that working in nursing homes in Lithuania and England was as different as day and night. I was told that in England the work was easier with more work tools and with a different approach to the patients.

It's true that employment conditions in England are different from those in Lithuania. However, after working for some time in England, I feel that the focus of the care system is the same – and it's the same around the world. Everywhere the goal is to care for the sick, the disabled, the frail and the elderly – to provide care for those who need it, whether through sickness or age.

Within England, I have found that the quality and attitude of managers varies from one nursing home or hospital to another. Everyone takes a different approach, whether it's a poor attitude or a nice one. Managing a nursing or medical environment is very difficult and stressful work, of course, but some managers make things worse by failing to care properly for their staff. For teamwork to be successful there needs to be a feeling of mutual respect.

While working in the Bupa nursing home, I had a clash with management that was caused – in my view – by my manager's negative attitude, and possibly her discrimination against foreigners. The disagreement centred around whether or not I should be allowed to work in a pair with another Lithuanian member of staff named Audrone. Like me, Audrone was a qualified nurse but she was starting out in England as a nursing assistant, and we soon became friends. I have already mentioned that we were required to work in pairs, but when Audrone and I were on the same shift, we were always separated. Instead, we were paired with nurses of other nationalities.

We told that we could never work together since we both were the same nationality and shared a native language other than English. For English employees, there was no such rule in force; the English staff were allowed to work together. Understandably, Audrone and I were upset, as we would have made a very good team.

It seems the decision was made to ensure that we didn't speak Lithuanian in front of the patients, which is quite understandable. However, the rule of only speaking English had already been made clear to us, and we were unlikely to break it. Indeed, from the very start, whenever we had spoken Lithuanian at work, we were told, "Speak English!"

I felt sure the problem could be solved more respectfully and did not require keeping us apart. I began to wonder if there was some other factor at play here. Was it perhaps discrimination against us as foreigners?

We began to feel some psychological pressure from some of the English staff members. We had done nothing wrong, but we were followed and kept under close observation. People were always watching how we conducted ourselves, and what we said to the nursing-home residents. We were warned that we could not talk to each other in our native language – even when we were not dealing with patients.

Our Indian nurse colleagues advised us that the rules being applied to Audrone and me were not correct. They told us not to tolerate such discrimination and to complain to the Bupa management. I agreed that what was happening was very wrong, and I had always known how to defend myself.

However, on this occasion I decided not to go running to the local Bupa office with my grievance. Instead, I called the nursing-home manager who was responsible for making this strange rule. I knew English well enough to speak with her, and I demanded an explanation, asking why she felt it was necessary to spy on me. She apologized and our discussion did not descend into an argument – but our relationship became cold.

Subsequently, she kept her distance from me and made no attempt to engage me in conversation. If she needed anything from me she would ask through other employees.

Audrone and I began to openly challenge the rule that nurses of the same national background could not work together, and suddenly everything turned upside down. They allowed us to work together, and all the hostility and discrimination ended.

Later on, an inspector from Bupa's head office visited, inviting me and Audrone for an interview together. She asked us if we had been treated well, if anyone had discriminated against us and if we were content in our work. Interestingly, she said nothing that led me to think that she was aware of our negative experiences. I said nothing to explain the unpleasant situation that Audrone and I had been through, and so the matter was never officially recorded. We were just happy to get on with our jobs without any unnecessary stress or bother.

Chapter VII

CLOSER TO MY GOAL

Through working at Bupa, I finally got my papers in order and gained a PIN number from the NMC. In other words, I obtained my license to work as a nurse in the UK. Now I was keen to get a nurse's job, and I felt my prospects were good. I had always tried to do everything correctly in my job. I had also made friends with both the nurses and patients. After all, the nursing assistant is the closest person to the patient, spending more time with them than anyone else.

Unfortunately, Bupa didn't offer me work as a nurse. After the situation with Audrone and the nursing-home manager, I think they didn't trust me. So, towards the end of my one-year contract in February 2007, I started to look elsewhere for work as a nurse. I found an agency in Birmingham that promised to help me take this important step. However, at that time, they could only get me work as a care assistant. English employers favour nurses who already have nursing experience in England – and this was one thing I lacked.

I decided to accept the care-assistant work that the agency offered me. However, I had not yet finished my one-year contract with Bupa, which meant I was doing both jobs at the same time for a while. I was in over my head and I found it a difficult balancing act.

The agency sent me to work in various nursing homes, residential homes, and hospitals, and I found myself working hard. The pressure was made worse by the fact that we often lacked sufficient personnel. However, I obtained some valuable experience in a wide range of settings, becoming better acquainted with both the work and with the nurses.

The harder you work, the better you understand not only your job, but also your potential, gaining increased confidence in your ability. I worked as a nursing auxiliary at both Birmingham and Walsall hospitals, and I soon realised that I was capable of succeeding at the next level. With this in mind, I sought the support of nursing colleagues in obtaining work as a qualified nurse.

I should perhaps say something about the daily routine in an English hospital. It starts the same way for both nurses and auxiliaries – with patient hygiene. The patients are washed and prepared for the day ahead, including getting dressed or into new nightclothes.

Later, the nurses hand out the medicines, while the auxiliaries take the patients' blood pressure, temperature and pulse. During all this, the staff talk to the patients, raising their mood. A kind word and a smile are as good as most medicines.

The nurses have a lot to organize, including patient consultations, doctors' visits, and various clinical procedures. Both nurses and care assistants are very busy and run around like hamsters on a wheel.

The British nursing system is quite complex, with various nursing grades and levels of independence, including chief nurses in hospitals, nurse practitioners working in GP clinics, and district nurses. Within hospitals, many nurses choose to specialize, developing and deepening particular skills as their careers progress.

When I first started working in British hospitals, I also came to learn of specialist jobs that I'd not encountered before, such as the phlebotomists, who take blood tests. To qualify as a phlebotomist, one does not need to be a nurse; one just takes several short courses and obtains a certificate. Then one can work in hospitals, GP clinics and blood transfusion stations. Some specialise in blood testing, while others give IV treatment to patients.

Good phlebotomy professionals are valued because their work is very responsible and difficult. There is a lot of skill involved in puncturing a vein correctly, as well as inserting cannulas. Due to this skill level, phlebotomists earn more than nursing assistants, although not as much as qualified nurses.

In one hospital, I remember being very surprised to read a message about the postponement of the insertion of a patient's IV drip because the phlebotomist was sick. The demand for phlebotomists in the UK is as high as for other nursing staff. However, recruitment of new phlebotomists requires proof of experience, and it is better if the experience is gained in the UK.

It was while working through the Birmingham agency that I began to understand the reasons why foreign workers were often distrusted. Most of them had come from Eastern European countries and they did not understand the British care system. These workers did not know the legal requirements of that system which could lead to complications and misunderstandings at times. Many of them were also unaware of their employment rights.

There had been articles in the Lithuanian press claiming that private nursing companies used Lithuanians as cheap labour. It's true that many Lithuanian care assistants were working for the minimum wage in the UK. However, this was true for people of all nationalities without exception, including people from India and the British staff.

I worked with people of many different nationalities during that period, some of whom were unfriendly or difficult, including several English and Filipino care assistants. It was the friendly women from India who always helped me and gave me advice. However, the nurses were all good-natured, and I made many long-term friends during that period.

Chapter IX

A NURSE AT LAST

I continued to seek that all-important first nursing job, and my persistence led me to a Wolverhampton nursing agency that was recruiting nursing staff of various sorts. I was invited to an interview with the agency's director, and after greetings and polite exchanges, we began a serious conversation about the profession.

My approach was based on my previous experiences and I was determined to let her know that I had been discriminated against and denied the trust that I deserved. I said I was having a hard time getting accepted as a nurse in England, and had been set to work only with other foreign nurses.

I asked: "What's the difference between me, a Pakistani or a Filipino nurse?"

I told her everything – that even though I was *upset* at that time, this should not detract from my ability to work as a nurse. But under no circumstances would I accept another care-assistant job.

After politely listening to me, the agency director calmly told me to ask questions that were not concerned with negatives, but related to the duties of a nurse.

I was ashamed and sorry for my unprofessional behaviour during my introduction. The rest of our conversation went very well, and I was over the moon when I was offered work as a qualified nurse in a nursing home.

I could not believe it when she said how much I would be paid by the hour. Since I did not understand the numbers completely, I thought that maybe I had heard incorrectly. In May 2007, I became a licensed nurse working in England.

Working through an agency suited me well, and I enjoyed the variety and flexibility it offered. Agency workers may be called upon to work at numerous care homes and hospitals, often moving quickly from one place to another. Key employees are called upon to fill gaps due to illness, annual leave or general staffing shortages. When managers find they are short of staff, they call the agencies and arrange for nurses or nursing assistants to be sent out. Agency staff are paid by the hour, and they may be called on to do many hours one week and very few the next.

However, they can also stipulate what sorts of work they are willing to do and what hours suit them best. During the nine years I worked in nursing homes, I was mostly able to pick those locations with a pleasant atmosphere and good staff. That does *not* mean this period of my life was uneventful; just about everything that could happen did happen. The work was not easy and there was a lot of responsibility on my shoulders. I was always being told to do everything by the book and document every step carefully. The words "Cover yourself" were always in the air.

I also worked a "bank nurse" during this period, which means working directly for the employer, but as a temporary worker with flexible hours. Nursing banks were set up to provide staff to fill staffing gaps, providing an alternative to the traditional nursing agency model. This was really good for me, because I was able to choose when I worked, with my schedule written out one week at a time. If I needed a night off, I just said that I couldn't work on that night. I also found it easier to travel to Lithuania or elsewhere on vacation.

The agencies also provided me with my first jobs caring for people in their own homes. These patients included the terminally ill, those with chronic debilitating conditions and the elderly.

The Wolverhampton agency that first hired me as a nurse subsequently closed down, but their staff went to other agencies, taking me with them. To this day, I am still working with my first director, although I am now working with my third agency. Employment-agency staff change and move on; they gain experience and connections and then open their own agencies. Very often they will stay in touch with nurses with whom they've built productive relationships. And so the circle turns.

I am now loyal to the Kare Plus agency, having worked for them since 2010. I like the team and the communication we have. However, much has changed since I was first offered a nursing job. At first, I was employed through the agency, but now I work as a subcontractor. In other words, I have my own personal business, and the agency hires me under contract. In the UK, many people work in this way.

I'm happy to say that, as I was advancing my nursing career in England, my husband was doing the same with his career as a doctor. When I was working with Bupa, he was working for the Staffordshire Ambulance Service on a six-month contract. In England, ambulance services of this kind employ professional paramedics, specially trained to respond to the scene of medical emergencies. However, in Staffordshire, the ambulance service was also employing doctors as part of their clinical team, going out to treat patients wherever required. My husband's station was the first and only ambulance station in England to make use of doctors in this way. There were three doctors employed there, all of them Lithuanians.

The programme for which my husband worked delivered both scheduled and unscheduled services across the West Midlands. He was greeted by the patients with gratitude and joy, receiving many thank-you letters from them. His work at Staffordshire was recognized for its excellence and professionalism, and he was awarded with certificates of gratitude and honour. I am very proud of him.

However, before his six months at Staffordshire were up, the agency from Lithuania that had promised to find him work invited him for an interview. He was successful, securing a new job as a disability assessor. The ambulance station asked him to stay on for another three-month period, and he agreed to do so, working both jobs simultaneously for a while, just as I had done previously. Finally, however, he waved goodbye to the ambulance service and settled into his new job. Today, he continues to follow his passion for medicine, working as an occupational health physician.

Chapter X

THE NURSING MERRY-GO-ROUND

Sometimes, working as a nurse feels like being on a merry-go-round: one is always moving, never still for a moment. Actually, the daily routine can be quite demanding, with plenty of stress to keep body and mind active.

Working hours vary greatly, but in a nursing home – where I've spent most of my time – the day shift is often from 8am to 8pm. Personally, I am more likely to start at 7:15am and finish around 9pm, so that's a very long day!

A typical working day begins with a short meeting or report, which we Lithuanians call a "five-minute". The nurses review each and every resident, including how they have been feeling and the details of the services/procedures provided.

We then look at our blogs and diaries to see what each resident needs in the coming day in terms of actions and procedures. This includes taking blood for blood tests that have been prescribed by the doctors. It might also involve

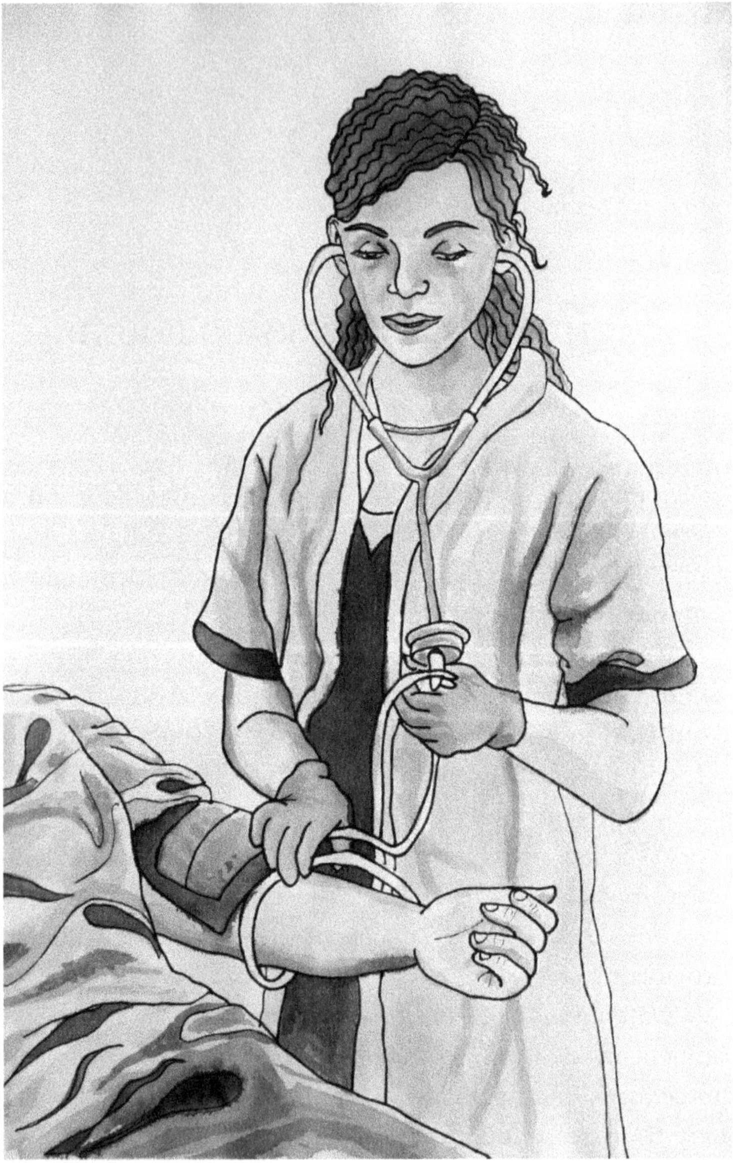

ordering medications, inviting a GP to see a resident, ordering a car for a resident to be referred to a specialist's consultation, or any number of other procedures or services. We nurses will be doing much of this while the care assistants are looking after the residents' more basic needs, such as washing, dressing and eating breakfast.

Medications are generally dispersed from 8am to 11.30am, although sometimes we might overrun by half an hour or so. If a care assistant notices the slightest change on a patient's body – such as a wound or bruise – they are required to tell the nurses. It is then up to the nurse to approach the patient, assess the situation and make decisions.

For example, if the problem is a sore, the nurse must decide if it is necessary to give treatment. Any treatment should be recorded in the nursing plan, while a photograph is taken, the problem reported to the administrator, the information faxed to the family doctor, and the relatives informed.

After completing the distribution of medicines, we nurses follow our diary, doing everything that is specified there. This includes everything relating to appointments, transfers, hospital visits, social workers, physiotherapist and doctors. After that, we might have a 20-minute break – if there's time.

At 1pm we serve lunch and hand out more medicines. Around 1:30pm or 2pm there is another meeting because around 2pm many of the employees are changing shifts. The nurse in charge provides information about the situation in her department and the entire team adjusts accordingly.

I really like teamwork. When I need to know something I only have to ask, and I get an answer straight away. The care assistants know almost everything.

We have 30 minutes for lunch, and at night, we get a rest break of one hour. After the lunch break, we write care plans containing many details and observations. During the course of the shift, I communicate with a wide range of colleagues, including physiotherapists, doctors, social workers, and other professionals who come to work with our residents. All of their observations are also recorded in the nurse's care plans and daily records.

Before 5pm, I start checking the blood of the diabetics. After which, it is time to administer insulin and other medicines during the "evening circle" routine. Some patients are fed through a feeding machine (PEG), and it is necessary to closely monitor the progress of this process to ensure a sufficient supply of liquids.

There are many different things we do that are not related to clinical treatment, but without which our relationships with the residents would be unimaginable. For example, sometimes a nurse becomes a beauty-shop employee – combing the residents' hair or putting cream on their faces. Sometimes you are simply a close friend – giving them a kiss at bedtime and wishing them sweet dreams.

We do not write such activities into our blogs, but it's our duty as caring human beings. It could not be otherwise. You just feel responsible for that person and for the duty that you as a nurse should perform.

There is quite a different system for working the night shift, which I sometimes do. The duties of a night nurse include the provision and reviewing of the existing stocks of medicines, as well as writing nursing plans. We also monitor various factors in the health of the residents, including nutrition, liquids and mucous membranes.

Mostly, though, I am on the day shift, where things are always in motion: ever circling and circling, never stopping. Nurses must take all their energy and share it with their colleagues and patients – and then find some more to share.

And just where does the strength come from? It should be said that nurses in the UK are not left without help. Seminars, training sessions and refresher courses are frequently provided, both through their employers and through umbrella organizations such as the Nursing and Midwifery Council. Nurses are taught new skills relating to patient care, management and broader skills, such as stress management. It's encouraging to know that, in Britain, the work of nurses is valued and their training is taken seriously.

Chapter XI

THE VARIETY OF LIFE

My work as an agency nurse has provided me with a great deal of variety, both in terms of working environments and the types of patients I've worked with. I have worked in residential care homes, nursing homes, private residences and homes for those suffering severe disabilities. While most of my patients have been elderly, there have also been quite a few middle-aged and younger people, including those who have suffered serious accidents. Some have been long-term residents with whom I've had the opportunity to build deeper relationships. Others have been passing through, in need of a period of recovery before moving on elsewhere. Meanwhile, many of those I've cared for have passed away, leaving behind grieving relatives – as well as being missed by the nurses and other staff.

Among the most rewarding categories of patient to work with is those who arrive at a nursing home in poor shape and leave it looking and feeling much better. Sometimes they come from hospital for a period of rehabilitation following a downturn in their health or some traumatic incident such as a fractured hip. They stay for six weeks before moving somewhere else, whether that be another nursing home, a residential care home or sheltered accommodation.

The term "rehabilitation" has different implications in different countries. In Lithuania, for example, rehabilitation often occurs in a sanatorium, which seems more like a hotel equipped with various spa treatments. There are massage and kineziotherapy (physiotherapy) treatments, often making use of the swimming pool. Patients perform exercises in water, take mineral and mud baths, relax in the jacuzzi and enjoy underwater massage. There are holistic therapies, such as aromatherapy and audiotherapy. Meanwhile, psychotheraphy is available for those who need it. The curative mud and mineral-water treatments depend on the deposits owned by the health resorts.

The range of spa services available in the Lithuanian system seeks to restore the patient's physical strength and bring back the joy of life.

While such a range of services is not normally available in the UK system, there are many effective rehabilitation services provided. For example, the physiotherapists in nursing homes help the patients greatly. I really admire the work they do, performing little miracles in facilitating the recovery of people who seemed hopeless. People come with mobility issues that prevent them from doing everyday tasks such as getting out from bed. But after six weeks, they often find the problem is solved, and they are able to walk about unaided. Finally, they go home with little help!

I have also worked with people suffering from serious disabilities, often the result of traumatic injuries such as traffic accidents. The institutions where these people reside are also called nursing homes, but the patients are often quite young. Our job as nurses and care assistants was to make these unfortunate people more comfortable and to bring them a better quality of life.

While rehabilitation does not always allow such people to walk out of the nursing home, we are able to brighten their lives in various ways. And for those who would be ending their lives in such a nursing home, it is our job to ensure their final days and hours are as easy and comfortable as possible. This focus on quality of life is one of the things I like most about the UK's health-care system.

I have also worked with people suffering from a range of chronic and debilitating diseases, which can affect both body and mind. Again, in addition to the purely clinical care, one of our chief responsibilities was to ensure an improved quality of life, wherever possible. Very often, a patient's day can be brightened simply be engaging in an interesting conversation with those around them. Like many care assistants and nursing staff, I have enjoyed many interesting conversations with such patients. They have shared their views and life stories, also teaching me about British life and habits. In this way, the patients have also helped to enrich my own quality of life.

Working with such people brought me some valuable life lessons too, including the importance of a positive – or at least accepting – attitude to life. I admired the fact that almost everybody was happy with the hand that Fate had dealt them. They gladly spoke about the achievements of their lives, no matter how small. In many cases, it was obvious that their lives had not been so great, but their complaints were far and few between.

Among the most debilitating conditions to strike people in later life are Alzheimer's disease and senile dementia. These conditions, which impair both memory and cognition, are very common throughout the world, and the UK is no exception. Aside from daily nursing care, such patients often need help with remembering things and remaining oriented, as well as dealing with the anxiety and panic that such conditions sometimes cause.

When I first started to work with patients suffering from Alzheimer's and senile dementia, I found myself suffering from huge emotional stress. It was not only the pressure of the work itself, but also the troubling thoughts that such an environment can provoke. I began to wonder at the point of life if it must end with such a hopelessly painful disease.

I witnessed their suffering up close and became very sensitive to their situation, filled with sorrow for these people who had lost their self-esteem.

As I got to know these patients, I learned more about their lives and all that they had experienced and accomplished. I saw the photos of their youth, filled with life, loving, caring and happiness. And now I could see them after disease had taken its toll, changing them forever. It caused a terrible pain in my heart and a feeling of hopelessness in my soul.

I began to realize that if it were not for the concern and compassion we nurses were able to provide, the emptiness in their lives might never be filled.

Chapter XII

NURSING AS A VOCATION

The profession of nursing wouldn't be what it is today if nurses felt they were doing a job like any other. In order to keep going back, day after day, year after year, they must feel the value of the service they provide to those in need. They must be committed to nursing as a vocation, a career choice based on compassionate motivations and with a proud history.

While working in England, I soon came to learn about Florence Nightingale, the English woman widely viewed as the founder of the modern nursing profession. She organized the treatment of wounded soldiers during the Crimean War in the 1850s, setting standards for nursing care that were the basis for the nursing profession. She and her team of nurses saved countless lives during the war, emphasising the importance of cleanliness and proper care for the sick and injured.

Thanks to an 1855 article in *The Times* newspaper, Nightingale gained the nickname "The Lady with the Lamp" for her tireless work during the Crimean War:

"She is a 'ministering angel' without any exaggeration in these hospitals, and as her slender form glides quietly along each corridor, every poor fellow's face softens with gratitude at the sight of her. When all the medical officers have retired for the night and silence and darkness have settled down upon those miles of prostrate sick, she may be observed alone, with a little lamp in her hand, making her solitary rounds."

She also went on to establish a school of nursing at St Thomas' Hospital in London, the world's first secular nursing school. The school has now been moved to Kings' College but it continues to provide high-quality nursing education. It inspired the spread of nursing schools around the world, many of which now provide bachelor's degrees and post-graduate qualifications in nursing studies.

Like many nurses, I find the story of Florence Nightingale inspiring, and her dedication and sense of vocation is just as relevant today as it ever was. Working in nursing homes, nurses and care assistants are exposed to a great deal of mental and emotional pressure. After all, the residents are nearing the end of their lives, which means they face both physical difficulties and the fears and regrets often associated with death.

It is often emotionally hard to look after people who are receiving end-of-life care, but we focus on carrying out the care plans for each resident, while offering them a caring and gentle attitude. While there are frequent difficulties, we can also see how our efforts are helping and it's gratifying when residents express their appreciation – as they often do.

After years as a nurse in nursing homes, I still love my work. I often feel more at home in my workplace than I do at home. I am so proud to be a member of this fine, caring profession, and I am confident that I know my job well, making me able to cope with just about any situation that arises.

I work long hours, sometimes 12 or 14 hours per day, and although I get tired, I am happy at the end of a shift that I have left the residents calm and happy. Since I spend so much time with the residents, I get to know their needs and personalities, and I often feel that I've become like a part of their extended family. I listen to their stories, as well as their aches and complaints, and I'm always mindful of my mission of helping those in need.

Many people learn of the work of doctors and nurses from watching TV shows and movies. From such dramas, it's clear how busy they are during the course of a working day. But what TV shows and movies can't communicate is the depth of feeling one has for a resident or patient suffering from a serious condition such as dementia or Alzheimer's disease. Nor indeed for those facing imminent death or breathing their last breaths. Nothing can communicate the depth of feeling that such situations evoke.

Of course, we have work to do, so we have to keep our feelings in check to some degree. In particular, we have to control our frustrations when we're called upon to comfort someone at 3am, when we'd rather be fast asleep ourselves. It's often in the early hours that a resident will have a bad dream and ask us to phone their son or daughter, or perhaps just offer some comfort and fluff up their pillows. And then there are those very trying moments when relatives get angry at you for something out of your control, perhaps shouting because you don't know when the consultant will be visiting.

Yes, this job would be all the more draining if we didn't view it as a vocation, a career that adds meaning to our lives. The days are long, and by the end, I just want to go home and relax in silence, without talking to anyone. The next morning comes and I prepare for work, calmly and happily anticipating another day – and I realize that I love my life and wouldn't want to change a thing.

Chapter XIII

BAD HABITS

There has been much debate about what factors shorten human lifespan. Among the conclusions is that the chief culprit is life-shortening bad habits. Yes, harmful habits are of great importance, and I have worked with many senior citizens who have suffered the consequences of irresponsible lifestyle choices.

One female patient once asked me if I smoked.

"No, I don't," I said. "I don't need it."

"Well, don't ever start smoking," she said. "See how painfully I pay for my weakness, how much I suffer for this bad habit."

This woman could clearly see the error of her ways. But there are many others who continue to smoke right up to the end of their lives, despite the harm this causes them. And we nurses are not permitted to stop them. Nursing homes even have smoking areas, and we must push them there in their wheelchairs to indulge their habit.

Another harmful lifestyle is that of the alcoholic. It is a habit that many people indulge even after they move into a nursing home. One often finds bottles of alcohol in the residents' rooms that have been brought there by relatives. Such things are not against the rules.

Some residents are given alcoholic drinks every evening. I remember the first time I saw this, and I found it hard to believe. It was an elderly woman who had whisky in hot water every evening during the evening tea break. When I saw this drink – known as a "hot toddy" – I was surprised, because I'd never come across it before. But I soon discovered that it's quite popular with older people in Britain.

Another woman had a glass of ginger wine each evening, and I would have to deliver it to her. Each time I brought the lady her wine, she gave me a lecture on how healthy the ginger was for her joints. She was suffering from arthritis and was unable to walk.

These two drinks are often seen as "winter warmers", and old ladies in particular enjoy their ginger wine.

Another patient would scream if we did not give her as much alcohol as she wanted. We had no time to argue with her, because we had to take care of the rest of the residents.

Generally speaking, we follow the philosophy that a person can use for their own pleasure anything they wish – and as much of it as they want. We nurses have to accept each person for what they are, warts and all.

Some residents are calm, thoughtful and well meaning, with good habits. Helping such people is relatively easy. However, there are many others whose bad habits or bad attitude can be trying, and that's when we have to make a special effort.

Some people have been spoiled throughout their lives, acting selfishly and always demanding more for themselves, regardless of the impact on others. Dealing with such people, we nurses must endure lots of whining and complaining. Sometimes our patience is drawn very thin, but then we stop, take an inspirational breath, count up to 10 – as psychologists teach us on courses – and try to gently continue performing our duties.

Other patients are difficult due to the nature of their condition. They may have an illness that affects their personality, causing confusion or anger, and in such cases they cannot be blamed for their bad actions. In such situations, a nurse can only be patient and offer to help.

This is the responsibility of the nurses – to provide assistance in old age without judging the patent or wondering how much they deserve from life. Everyone has the right to good nursing care in old age.

Chapter XIV

THE DESIRE TO LIVE

One evening I had to speak with one of the residents of the nursing home where I worked. He was over 80 years old and his words were strained. Every one of his words spoke of weakness and despair; it was as if he was no longer among the living. He complained that his life no longer made sense and that he was no longer needed.

"We are born, we grow up, we raise children; then we get older, we become a burden to ourselves, and finally a burden to others – and this is the end," he said.

I realized that the man had abandoned his desire to live because he felt useless to everyone. As long as he had felt needed, he was able to enjoy nature, the sun and the blue sky, remembering the most beautiful moments of his life. Winter would come, but he would wait for spring, keen to continue living. But once he felt he was no longer needed, the hope and desire to live vanished – and the end was not far away.

It's a shame, but a lot of people think like this man. Their strength, health, beauty, and eyesight have been lost; their body no longer responds to their wishes; they are no longer themselves. And so they give up.

But should we give up? Should we just stop and go away? If so, what was the meaning of coming into this world in the first place?

In Britain, the elderly rarely feel useless, and no one ever thinks of them as such. As an outsider arriving in Britain, I found it remarkable that senior citizens were out in their cars and shuffling into the store with their walking frames. In Lithuania, by contrast, I have never seen the senior citizens, especially the elderly women, being so independent. In the UK, it is commonplace and of no surprise to anyone. I really like this form of respect.

This approach helps to maintain a sense of purpose and usefulness in life, which can in turn help to prolong life.

The 19th century American philosopher, poet, and essayist Ralph Waldo Emerson addressed this point when he wrote: "We do not count a man's years until he has nothing else to count."

I'll always remember one old lady whose optimism I admired. She enjoyed life and was very active. In as much as she was able, she participated in the life of the Church and was engaged in charity work. When her fingers were able to move, she knitted blankets that the Church donated to deprived people. I can imagine how much love and good wishes that old woman put into the covers that she made. There seems to be something miraculous about such an attitude. I admired her and I admire people like her.

There is no such thing as a definite point beyond which death is inevitable. Any such limits can be shifted, depending on how we live our lives. The more active and meaningful a person's life is, the further the limits move forward, becoming blurred, until they disappear.

There are many elderly women who knits gloves, scarves and blankets for charity. Those items are so beautiful! These women believe in their strength; they ask the nurses to bring pain-relief medicines – and then they continue to work. They are filled with ideas on how to help others and a willingness to put them into action. That type of old age is really a blessed old age.

Actually, far from being depressing, old age can be a time of inspiration for some lucky people. Toward the end of their life, some people are able to reflect on the wisdom they've accumulated and to share this with their children and grandchildren.

This is an idea emphasized by Joseph Murphy, the American cleric, preacher and philosopher, who said: "Age is not the flight of years; it is the dawn of wisdom in the mind of man."

Old age is not necessarily a tragedy. It is just an inevitable part of life, and it has always been that way. Old age is just a physical change in the body, a new step forward in our lives. It does not diminish what a person has had during the course of their life: beauty, wisdom, talent, strength, compassion, and many other wonderful attributes. There are many forces in the human mind that are stronger than the merely physical.

Chapter XV

RAISING THE SPIRITS

One of the more satisfying tasks of a nurse in a nursing home is helping with leisure activities aimed at lifting the spirits of the residents. This includes activities that residents would have enjoyed in their younger days: everything from singing and dancing, through to drawing pictures and playing games. This provides them with some enjoyable ways of passing the time, as well as reminding them of the happy times from their past.

Sometimes singers will visit a nursing home. They sing old songs and the patients remember them, often singing along together. Dancers also visit, encouraging residents to join them in dancing to tunes that they knew in their youth. The aim is the same: to raise the spirits of the old and sick.

Sometimes there is a visit by a mini-zoo, allowing residents a chance to stroke friendly animals, such as dogs, rabbits and guinea pigs. At the home where I work, there is a soft, fluffy rabbit. He is loved by all the residents, and especially by those who are unable to leave their beds.

There are also visits by Church representatives, who help to nurture the residents' religious faith. This is particularly useful for those who find it difficult to leave the nursing home for visits to church.

Most people like bingo games. A special machine is used to randomly select the numbers, and the residents mark these off their bingo cards. If one of them is lucky enough to get all the right numbers, they win the prize. It is a simple game, but it gives the residents a lot of fun and puts them in a good mood.

During various festive occasions, charity raffles are held, with the prizes often donated by nursing-home employees and the relatives and friends of patients. Staff and patients buy tickets for a nominal price, often just one pound. Everyone who has bought a ticket will wait with eager interest, keen to see who breaks out in a smile, a sure sign of success.

Sunday is movie day. Residents get to watch old films that they've loved. The stories, the actors and the music all take them back to happier times.

In combination, these various activities remind residents of the joy and fulfilment they experienced in the past, showing them that the same feelings can be re-kindled in the present. It's a valuable lesson, and it can work wonders to blow away the blues.

At the nursing home where I currently work, some of the residents are very talented. For example, we have a talented artist. His paintings are hanging on the walls of his room. Since he had a stroke, he can no longer draw, but he still uses his pencil to colour children's books. I like to sit with him and watch him working, colouring the pictures.

He tells the stories of the origins of his paintings, what he painted and where. He talks about his sources of inspiration for each piece, including the people that he knew at the time. Such discussions are enjoyable for us both.

Although they may not be so talented, most residents at the home take part in drawing lessons at some point. During one such session, one woman drew two smileys inside a heart, and with a bright-eyed expression, she said to me: "Here are you and me."

I was very excited and thanked her. In the evening, when I came to wish her a good night, I found her holding that picture and kissing it.

Another woman stricken with Parkinson's disease was happy to have created a postcard. I complimented her and she became even happier. She wrote some wonderful words on the postcard: "All you need is love." These were sensitive words, and very true.

It's great to see people forget about their age, focusing instead on gathering together all the good things of their life, getting every last drop of joy out of life – right down to the last drop in the well. In this respect, nurses often act as guardian angels for their patients, helping them live life to the full.

Chapter XVI

THE POWER OF LOVE

Even at the sunset of life, even in the nursing homes, people find each other, fall in love and become couples. One couple in particular stands out in my memory: an elderly woman had lost her gift of speech after a stroke, while her male friend was over 90 years old. They really loved each other and wanted to get married. Their dream was interrupted by the man's death, but I believe that he left life happy, because until the last minute he felt responsible for the woman that Destiny had brought his way.

I remember another married couple who showed the power of love. The woman was disabled and the husband would come and visit her in the nursing home. Their faces would shine brightly with love when they met – a sort of radiance that I'd never seen before. It's hard to believe that a man could love a woman like that.

Having lived together for more than 60 years, this couple had often talked happily about their children, where they had worked and what they had achieved throughout their lives. And now, even though the wife could no longer speak, they still had the ability to communicate. I really believe that the language they spoke to one another was the language of mutual love and understanding.

Another lasting relationship illustrated the value of love as a source of strength. One morning, I was bringing medicines to the residents as they sat in their armchairs, when I found myself in a funny situation. A man came to visit one of the women sitting there. He shouted out: "Well, how is the most beautiful girl in the world?"

His voice was full of joy, and I thought for a moment that the compliment was meant for me. But this was a mistake on my part. The man walked past me, went directly to his wife and kissed her. These words – the nicest, warmest of words – were for the love of his life.

"How beautiful!" I thought.

Those loving words made life worth living for them both. I knew that throughout the whole year, that deep feeling of mutual love allowed them to keep enjoying life.

Chapter XVII

LIFE AND DEATH

Working in a nursing home, I often get to know residents very well – learning many details about their long and interesting lives – only to find that I have to say a final farewell at the end.

My job involves lots of talking and listening, and many patients have told me the stories of their lives and loved ones. Very often, their children had emigrated to places like Canada, Australia, the USA and other countries. This has increased their opportunities for travel, but it has also put distance between themselves and those they love.

People have related to me the joyful and wonderful moments of their lives. Through their stories, I travelled to many distant parts of the world. Many patients provided vivid accounts of their experiences and impressions. They also offered me advice on where to go, where to stay and what to see. I have travelled a lot with my husband, and I have much to tell my patients as well. We have often enjoyed sharing the experiences and impressions of our various travels and adventures.

I have been glad to hear stories of the loving relationships that have brought happiness to my patients, as well as the various accomplishments of which they're proud. It's good to share in other people's sense of satisfaction.

However, our exchanges have often had their sad side as well, and I have listened to many heart-breaking life experiences. Some of these patients were nearly one hundred years old, with no relatives to confide in, and so whatever sadness they felt was shared with the nursing staff. I often became tired of listening and felt a hidden grief for their loneliness. There were moments when I wanted to cry.

Once, I asked a very old lady, "Would you like some painkillers?"

She answered, "Nurse, I'd rather you brought me a pill for death."

She didn't mean a pill to cure death, of course, but one to hurry it along.

Nurses are generally reluctant to talk with patients about death. It is a painful and sensitive subject. The end of life is inevitable, but every patient has different ways of dealing with this fact. Some people are tired of living; they are sad, waiting for the end, immersed in apathy. Others take a more positive approach; they are able to be philosophical and enjoy life until the last moment – that final farewell.

Even so, it is never easy to say goodbye to those patients for whom I've cared, building a close relationship over time. Watching someone you care for slip away is difficult, although one can perhaps take comfort in the knowledge that they went out quietly, without pain, and without regrets.

In a way, death brings an additional burden for the care assistants and nursing staff. Due to our responsibilities, we must remain strong, even when we feel very sad. We may feel like crying at the death of someone we've cared for, but we know we must be strong for the sake of those around us. We must be strong and get on with the next task on the list.

At first, whenever I lost one of my patients or residents, I would get very upset. I would wonder about the meaning of life if it only ends in death. What was the point of all their hard work and struggling if it ends this way?

But over the years my attitude has changed. These days, I always think that the person who died has gone to a better world – and I pray for them.

Chapter XVIII

MORE THAN JUST WORK

Writing this book has enabled me to speak with nurses and care assistants working in a wide range of specializations, including care for the disabled, oncology and dementia nursing. Many of them have told me of their experiences in Britain's health sector, both in private institutions and the National Health Service. Much of what they say rings true for me, and so I have dedicated this chapter and the following one to sharing their stories and observations.

Two of the nurses featured here are British, while the other two have come from abroad, just like me. There is huge demand for professional nurses and care assistants in Britain's health sector. The greatest demand is from Australia, New Zealand, Canada and Europe, including such nations as Poland, Russia and Lithuania.

Just like me, many of them have found employment through nursing agencies, securing positions in hospitals, nursing homes, care homes, as well as in the patients' personal homes. They have also benefited from the training provided by such agencies, helping them to adapt to the British health system and progress their careers.

While working with one employer, I met a Russian nurse called Nina who became a good friend. For the past ten years Nina has worked as a support worker with two boys with learning difficulties, caring for them in their own specially adapted house provided by the local authorities.

Nina shares the work with two other people, each working a 24-hour shift before handing over to the next one. Nina describes her work as both useful and interesting. As always in life, she has faced a variety of interesting situations, some funny and others more serious, and she has immortalized these experiences in a book.

Here are a few comments from Nina on her work:

"I have been working with them for 10 years. My time with them has become part of my life. It is not just work. We are friends. I not only do all the household work in their homes, we spend quality time together; going to the pool, attending a variety of events, we go for recreation, even fishing. This is an invaluable experience.

"I wrote a book about these guys and told funny stories that happened during our communication time. I am glad that this country cares for its disabled citizens and gives them an opportunity to live a full life, without feeling that they are different."

Among the many employers dealing in specialised areas of nursing is Marie Curie, a charity that provides care at home for patients with terminal illness. This enables disabled, sick and very weak or elderly patients to stay in their homes and get expert help, not only for their maladies but also for the practical and psychological needs of their relatives.

Among the Marie Curie nurses I have met is a British woman called Elizabeth. She is a Registered Mental Nurse and she shares some of her thoughts below:

"I like to work with seriously ill patients individually, so the patient can receive qualified assistance around the clock. This is serious psychological work and a big responsibility for the nurse. The knowledge that I am helping a person spend the last days of life quietly, with dignity and without pain is the redeeming quality of my job. Caring for a dying person has a particular responsibility for the nurse and is a huge experience for the family.

"There is a big difference, for the patient receiving care, between a nursing home or hospital, on the one hand, and his or her natural environment at home, on the other. It is a huge privilege for the nurse to be able to take care of the sick in their homes and communicate with their families."

Another nurse with a fascinating story is Susan, an English woman who works as a dementia nurse through the charity Dementia UK. Nurses working for the organization are called "Admiral Nurses" in honour of the charity's founder, Joseph Levy, who was a keen sailor.

Susan became a specialist dementia nurse after years of personal experience caring for her parents. Her mother suffered from Parkinson's disease and eventually died. Later, her father was diagnosed with Lewy body dementia, and

Susan took on responsibility for his care. These personal experiences helped Susan to understand the difficulties of living with dementia and also the emotional strain of providing care.

Below she describes her experiences in her own words, as originally published on the Dementia UK website:

'Looking back to being a carer, I can remember feeling totally baffled about my Dad's dementia. I don't remember his diagnosis being explained to me at any time. He experienced visual and tactile hallucinations which did not disturb him, merely intrigued him. He would see people lining up in our living room to look at the pictures on our walls and he was most concerned about the fact that they had not paid an entrance fee to come in!

'Dad also used to get up in the night and look for the 'small children' who used to pinch him whilst he sat in his chair. Many a night was spent with him upending the living room furniture. I did not hear him, but when I got up in the morning I would find a mess and sometimes he would be sitting or lying on the floor amongst it. Our relationship suffered, because I didn't understand what he was experiencing.

'One morning, I found Dad on the floor again and I was at my wits' end. I just sobbed; I didn't know how to handle it any more. Dad, in a moment of clarity, said, 'I think I should go somewhere where I could be looked after and you won't have to worry about me so much.' Part of me was happy he felt able to consider a home and part of me was thinking, 'Don't you want me to look after you anymore?'

'Dad moved into a nursing home not far away, so it was easy to visit him – well, travel-wise at least. Dad didn't like the home during the first couple of weeks but he soon settled. He actually flourished,

blossoming with the attention he got, much more than I could give him – frazzled and desperate as I was. I was able to spend some quality time with him and our relationship changed for the better.

"One thing that I have learnt from personal and professional experience is that when a loved-one moves into a care home, it does not always solve all the problems. The guilt that I felt was indescribable, even though the idea had partially been at my Dad's suggestion. I felt empty, sick, and ashamed. It took a long time for those feelings to subside, even though I knew that it was the best thing for both of us. This experience is helpful because I know what emotions carers are experiencing, because I have had first-hand experience."

Chapter XIX

NURSE GALINA

Another person who has related her experiences to me is the Russian nurse Galina, who came to England in 1999. She originally made a career for herself in Russia, training as a doctor and treating people with tuberculosis. She wrote her dissertation, debated it and became a Doctor of Science. However, she was not content to pursue a career as a physician in Russia, preferring instead to seek a new life abroad.

She had her mind set on learning English, so she decided to come to England. There, she met her future husband, got married and settled down. Initially, Galina worked in a shop, but she later found employment as a tutor of the Russian language – a job that she continues to this day.

Medicine was still her big passion though, and she hoped to put her training to good use in England. However, she soon discovered that medical diplomas from countries outside the European Union are not recognized in the UK.

If she wanted to continue her work as a TB specialist, Galina would have to resume her medical studies in England, passing yet more exams.

Instead, she decided to undergo training as a nurse. She easily completed her Postgraduate Diploma in Nursing Studies at Nottingham University, obtaining credits for many of her medical studies in Russia. She was encouraged to continue studying and qualify as a doctor in the UK, but she was content to embark on a nursing career.

In 2014, after several years of nursing, Galina became a Success Coach, using the "Thinking Into Results" system designed by Bob Proctor. She now organizes entrepreneurship seminars for all professions, including nursing staff and doctors. She provides this training in parallel with her clinical responsibilities as a hospital nurse.

Below, she relates her experiences as a nurse in the British health sector, including work practices, professional values and comparisons with her experiences in the Russian system where she first trained:

"I have worked in a hospital in England at the post-operative surgical block section since 2008. This is a section where patients wake up after surgical procedures, and my duty is to monitor their condition after their surgery. The first hours after an operation are very important. When the patients wake up, I check their pulses, blood pressure, and body reactions. If all is well and all the tests are good, I then send the patient to receive treatment in accordance with the proper diagnosis section. This is a very interesting and responsible job.

"Our hospital has eight operating theatres: orthopaedic, gynaecological, abdominal cavity, urology, surgery of the jaw, and miscellaneous, which carries out various other operations. There are no such departments in Russian hospitals. At first, I did not understand why the nurses were needed there. In Russian hospitals, after surgery, patients are transported to the intensive-care unit, and immediately after, the patient is discharged for treatment at home.

"England's hospitals are very different from Russian hospitals. First of all – size. You can get lost in an English hospital very quickly. The hospital is like a city. Around the hospital are huge parking lots, a cafe, information offices, a games room for children, a hair salon, and other service agencies.

"All hospital rooms, wards, corridors, and procedural rooms are very clean, and because they are regularly cleaned, there is rarely a case of staphylococcus. It is obviously not like this in Russia.

"Nurses' and doctors' interpersonal communication relationships in England and Russia are very different. England's doctors highly appreciate the nurse's opinions and advice. The nurses have the right to tell the doctor why they do not agree with treatment and what they expect from the doctor to help improve the patient's condition. Doctors are friendly with all the staff, and are prepared to accept their advice. Of course, there are exceptions, which depend upon human culture, education, and manners.

"An anaesthesiologist from Russia worked with us. One male nurse did not respect this doctor. Not because the doctor did not have enough professionalism, but because he did things different from what was accepted in our hospital. In England, it's normal for every hospital to have its own rules, treatment tactics, document management, and

more. Our hospital managers are very radical and resistant to change. Workers who come from other hospitals are required to work by the new hospital's routines and principles. The establishment is always afraid of something new, even if it would improve on some of their possibly out-dated methods.

'The working relationship between the nurses, other nurses and the staff are usually friendly and polite, although sometimes, as everywhere, there are misunderstandings, complaints and gossip. The British are very fond of complaining. Each hospital has special sections dedicated to dealing with complaints. If you are unhappy enough, you can fill in a complaint form and send it to the complaints department. I have never done it, because in general I do not like to complain, and I have never heard a complaint that warranted a formal filing.

'The nurses are divided into levels and categories. There are seven levels. Like most ordinary nurses, I got on the fifth level. The sixth level includes managers, and the highest includes section and hospital executives.

'Doctors visit patients in the morning, make recommendations and then leave. If necessary, the nurse will call a doctor. So the whole department really rests upon the nurses' shoulders. Nurses work long hours, usually from 7 am to 8 pm. They have to not only carry out their direct duties, but also write in detail in their nursing blogs. If everything has not been written down during your shift, you must stay after your 13 hours of shift work and finish processing your records. Luckily, the section where I work does not have much paperwork, and that makes me happy.

'My relationships with my colleagues are nice and respectful, even though sometimes I hear hints about my accent, my culture, or from where I came; but most often I take them as simple jokes, and

everything passes without conflict. My relationships with the doctors are also nice. Many doctors from other countries – like India, Pakistan, Egypt, Iran, Hungary, the Netherlands and Ireland – work at the hospital. I have met doctors from Lithuania and Latvia, but only one doctor from Russia.

"In England, staff training is very serious. Every year we attend organized conferences in which we are reminded of our rights and our responsibilities in the hospital. Vocational training on how to properly wash hands, what to look for to notice signs of sepsis, activities and protocol surrounding blood transfusions. We are taught to handle documents, warned not to leave them in public, and recently we were given a course on how to recognize terrorists and where to call if we are suspicious of someone. The staff are also familiarized with the latest documents, but the most important training is how to resuscitate people.

"Patients are generally kind. Especially pleasing are the elderly; always smiling, always a 'thanks' for the service, no matter how small. The younger patients are less appreciative and polite. They are more demanding and straightforward and like to complain and demand better service. Sometimes I have the desire to send them to a Russian hospital, or even better to the Russian village hospital, so that they can compare the conditions and help there with what they are getting in England.

"In England, hospital patient services are very good. We have all that is necessary for diagnosis and treatment and there are a variety of antibiotics, painkillers and a variety of symptomatic drugs. Patients do not need to bring anything from home.

"I will never forget my first impression while giving birth in Nottingham Hospital. It was the first time I had been in an English hospital and it all seemed like a fairy tale. I could not believe that it could be like that. My husband was always with me, and to me it seemed

like a miracle. In Russia, men are not allowed to participate during the birth of their children. In the birthing room there was even a TV, and my husband watched cricket matches between contractions. And if you can believe it, there's a great coincidence. My son is a great cricket player – and it's his favourite sport!

"Every minute, nurses came into the delivery room and asked how I felt, or if I wanted an anaesthetic, or something else. Soon after giving birth, they brought me a phone to call my parents in Russia to announce the good news. An interesting coincidence: on the same day, May 20th, the son of British Prime Minister Tony Blair was born. I gave birth to my second son in the same hospital. Only, the second time I was less surprised. How quickly we get used to something good!

"When my second son was born, my mother was visiting me, and she and my husband and elder son came into the ward to visit me and her grandchild. My mother was absolutely surprised that it was so easy to come from the street into the ward to see her daughter with child! I was released home on the second day after giving birth. I felt so good that I was able to get behind the wheel of a car and to go pick up my eldest son from kindergarten."

Chapter XX

FINAL THOUGHTS

Looking back on my long journey from Latvia to life as a qualified nurse in England, I feel a great sense of accomplishment. Of course, many people have made similar journeys, but that does not lessen the importance of each individual journey.

My own story started with a dream, followed by another, and another. And finally, all of my dreams have come true. Now I am doing the job that I love in a country that has been good to me, providing work and a comfortable life for me and my husband.

This book is also the result of a dream: to share my experiences, not only as a migrant, but as someone who has witnessed a great deal of human suffering and done her best to alleviate it. I only hope that my readers will find something within these pages that interests and perhaps inspires them.

The training of a nurse is complex and difficult, and the daily routine can be exhausting. But no matter how competent you are in technical terms, this will never be enough if you fail to inject genuine caring into your work.

Particularly with the old and chronically ill, there is a need for tenderness, for extra care, for listening, and for making a difference. When the patient opens their eyes and sees a nurse or care assistant, their pain lessens. The patient always welcomes the nurse because the nurse makes the patient's life more meaningful.

Nursing staff must always try to be pleasant, speaking kind and comforting words wherever possible. And yes, this relieves pain. So say most patients.

As a nurse, if you love your work, wherever the patient lives also becomes your own home. Likewise, the patients themselves become your family.

I am proud of working as a nurse in the UK. I am grateful to Fate and to God for the fact that everything came together. I am grateful that I found myself here, in this place.

IT IS MY DUTY

Dawn Butler, RN
(Pennsylvania)

I walk through those doors with pride,
Who's life will i save tonight?
Someone is waiting for me,
Someone is alive today because of my duty.
Sometimes we cry cause we can't save them all,
God sometimes won't let us interfere when he calls.
A baby's first breath when he looks at me,
The joy of my first delivery.
The tear i wipe a way with my own hands,
The life ending of a gentle old man.
The night seems so dark and the morning so bright.
Being a nurse you see life in a different light.
Who will i save tonight?
Who will hold my hand during their last breath with no fright?
Who will enter this world on my shift?
How many mothers will greet their babies with a kiss?
I don't know who these special people are
but i will meet them with every call
I will hold them tight and help the pain
I will hold them up when they feel faint.
I will be strong when i am needed
That is my job, I am a nurse..that is my duty.

Lightning Source UK Ltd.
Milton Keynes UK
UKHW041521240219
337912UK00001B/10/P

9 781910 886922